KOI POND SECRETS

Design, Stocking, and Maintenance for Vibrant Aquatic Life

Danso Opoku

Table of Contents

1 5

INTRODUCTION 6

WHY KOI PONDS ARE MORE THAN JUST A HOBBY 8

A GATEWAY TO MINDFULNESS 9

THE JOY OF KOI KEEPING 11

HOW TO USE THIS GUIDE..15

CHAPTER ONE 19

THE ART OF KOI PONDS 19

A BRIEF HISTORY OF KOI PONDS................................19

UNDERSTANDING KOI BEAUTY, BEHAVIOR, AND SYMBOLISM 20

TYPES OF KOI FISH AND THEIR UNIQUE APPEAL............22

DESIGNING YOUR DREAM KOI POND...........................23

CHOOSING THE PERFECT LOCATION 24

DETERMINING THE RIGHT SIZE AND DEPTH 25

POND STYLES NATURAL VS FORMAL DESIGNS...............26

CHAPTER TWO 29

BUILDING A KOI POND 29

TOOLS AND MATERIALS NEEDED 29

STEP-BY-STEP GUIDE TO POND CONSTRUCTION 31

ENSURING PROPER WATER FLOW AND CIRCULATION ..34

TIPS FOR DIY ENTHUSIASTS VS HIRING PROFESSIONALS 35

STOCKING YOUR POND WITH KOI...................36

HOW TO SELECT HEALTHY KOI FISH...............37

INTRODUCING KOI TO THEIR NEW HOME SAFELY.........38

UNDERSTANDING KOI SOCIAL BEHAVIOR AND HIERARCHY 40

THE RIGHT NUMBER OF KOI FOR YOUR POND SIZE.......41

CHAPTER THREE 43

MAINTAINING OPTIMAL WATER QUALITY.....................43

THE IMPORTANCE OF OXYGENATION AND AERATION ..45

ROUTINE WATER CHANGES AND TESTING 46

ALGAE CONTROL AND PREVENTING WATER CLOUDINESS 47

FEEDING YOUR KOI 49

NUTRITIONAL REQUIREMENTS FOR HEALTHY KOI 50

CHOOSING THE RIGHT FOOD PELLETS, TREATS, AND SEASONAL DIETS 52

FEEDING SCHEDULES AND QUANTITY RECOMMENDATIONS...54

COMMON FEEDING MISTAKES TO AVOID 55

LANDSCAPING AROUND YOUR POND 58

ADDING PLANTS FOR SHADE AND BEAUTY 58

AQUATIC PLANTS FOR NATURAL FILTRATION 60

CREATING A HARMONIOUS ECOSYSTEM WITH NATIVE FLORA 62

PROTECTING YOUR POND FROM PREDATORS 64

CHAPTER FOUR 68

SEASONAL CARE FOR YOUR KOI POND 68

PREPARING YOUR POND FOR WINTER 68

SPRING CLEANING AND RESTARTING THE POND SYSTEM 70

MANAGING HEAT AND EVAPORATION IN SUMMER 73

FALL MAINTENANCE REMOVING LEAVES AND DEBRIS .. 75

KOI HEALTH AND DISEASE PREVENTION 77

RECOGNIZING SIGNS OF ILLNESS OR STRESS 78

COMMON KOI DISEASES AND TREATMENTS 80

QUARANTINE PROCEDURES FOR NEW FISH 83

TIPS FOR KEEPING KOI STRESS-FREE AND HEALTHY 85

CHAPTER FIVE 88

ENHANCING YOUR KOI POND EXPERIENCE 88

ADDING LIGHTING FOR EVENING AMBIANCE 88

BUILDING BRIDGES, SEATING, AND PATHWAYS 91

INCORPORATING FISH FEEDING STATIONS....................93

HOSTING KOI POND TOURS OR COMPETITIONS............95

TROUBLESHOOTING AND FAQS 97

HOW TO FIX A LEAKING POND.....................................100

WHAT TO DO IF KOI ARE JUMPING OR HIDING 102

ANSWERS TO COMMON BEGINNER QUESTIONS.........104

CELEBRATING YOUR KOI POND SUCCESS....................106

THE TRANQUILITY AND FULFILLMENT OF KOI KEEPING
....107

INSPIRING STORIES FROM THE KOI COMMUNITY 109

INTRODUCTION

Imagine stepping into your backyard to find a tranquil oasis brimming with the vibrant colors of koi swimming gracefully in crystal-clear water. The soothing sound of a waterfall, the gentle rustle of aquatic plants, and the serenity of the scene offer a daily escape into nature. A koi pond is more than a decorative feature—it's a harmonious blend of art, science, and passion, bringing life and beauty to your outdoor space.

In Koi Pond Magic, we'll take you on a journey to create and sustain a thriving koi pond, whether you're an experienced pond enthusiast or a curious beginner. This book is your comprehensive guide to building a stunning pond, selecting the perfect koi, and maintaining an environment where they can flourish. We begin by exploring the fundamentals of pond construction, including choosing the right location, designing for both function and beauty, and understanding the essential equipment needed to maintain water quality. Next, we'll dive into the fascinating world of koi, covering everything from selecting healthy fish to understanding their behaviors, dietary needs, and seasonal care.

But it doesn't stop there. A healthy koi pond is a living ecosystem that requires balance and dedication. You'll learn about maintaining water quality, preventing common issues like algae blooms, and safeguarding your koi from predators and diseases. Along the way, we'll share tips and insights to ensure your pond becomes a long-lasting source of joy and pride. Whether you dream of a serene garden retreat or a lively pond that captures the admiration of all who visit, this book provides the knowledge and inspiration to bring your vision to life. Get ready to unlock the magic of koi ponds and transform your outdoor space into a haven of peace and beauty.

WHY KOI PONDS ARE MORE THAN JUST A HOBBY

At first glance, koi ponds might seem like an elaborate backyard project or a pastime for fish enthusiasts. But the truth is, koi ponds are far more than just a hobby. They are a fusion of art, nature, and mindfulness, offering profound benefits that enrich your life in unexpected ways.

A Living Work of Art

A koi pond is a dynamic masterpiece that evolves with time. From the glistening water to the vibrant koi fish gliding through it, every element contributes to a serene and visually stunning environment. The addition of aquatic plants, natural rocks, and carefully designed landscaping turns your pond into a tranquil escape, reflecting your creativity and connection to nature.

A GATEWAY TO MINDFULNESS

The soothing sound of water, the graceful movements of koi, and the gentle rustle of nearby foliage create a meditative atmosphere. Spending time near a koi pond provides a moment of calm in a hectic world, allowing you to recharge and find peace. It's a daily reminder to slow down, breathe deeply, and appreciate the beauty around you.

An Ecosystem in Harmony

Koi ponds are thriving ecosystems, requiring a balance of water quality, plant life, and aquatic creatures. Managing this delicate equilibrium fosters an appreciation for the interconnectedness of life. Watching your koi thrive as a result of your care brings a sense of fulfillment and accomplishment that extends beyond the pond.

A Connection to Tradition and Culture

Koi ponds have deep roots in Japanese culture, symbolizing prosperity, perseverance, and harmony. Owning a koi pond connects you to these timeless traditions, adding a layer of meaning to your outdoor space. Each koi fish, with its unique colors and patterns, tells its own story, enriching your understanding of this ancient art.

A Gathering Place

A koi pond isn't just a personal retreat; it's a magnet for conversation and connection. Family, friends, and neighbors are naturally drawn to the beauty and tranquility of your pond. Whether it's a quiet moment shared with a loved one or a lively discussion about the pond's design and inhabitants, koi ponds create lasting memories.

More Than a Hobby

Koi ponds blend creativity, responsibility, and relaxation into a unique experience that transcends mere pastime. They inspire mindfulness, provide a sense of achievement, and cultivate a deeper connection to nature and culture. In a koi pond, you don't just build something beautiful—you nurture a living, breathing sanctuary that feeds your soul.

THE JOY OF KOI KEEPING

Koi keeping is more than a pastime; it's an enriching journey that brings beauty, tranquility, and a sense of fulfillment into your life. The allure of koi goes beyond their vibrant colors and graceful movements—it lies in the connection they create between you, nature, and the calming rhythm of the aquatic world.

A Burst of Living Color

Koi are often called "living jewels," and for good reason. Their dazzling hues and intricate patterns turn any pond into a mesmerizing display of nature's artistry. Watching these elegant creatures glide effortlessly through the water is a simple yet profound pleasure that never loses its charm.

A Personal Connection

Koi aren't just decorative; they are interactive and intelligent beings. Over time, they come to recognize their caregivers and may even feed from your hand, creating a unique bond. This personal connection transforms koi keeping from a hobby into a rewarding relationship.

A Gateway to Relaxation

There's something inherently soothing about koi ponds. The gentle ripples of water, the delicate movements of fish, and the serene environment create a peaceful retreat from the stresses of daily life. Spending even a few minutes observing your koi can help reduce anxiety and promote mindfulness.

A Celebration of Growth

From selecting young koi to watching them mature into vibrant, healthy adults, koi keeping is a journey of growth. As you learn to care for their needs—maintaining water quality, providing a balanced diet, and creating a safe habitat—you'll find joy in seeing your efforts reflected in their vitality and beauty.

A Window into Nature's Wonders

Koi keeping fosters a deeper appreciation for the delicate balance of life. A koi pond is its own ecosystem, requiring attention to water chemistry, plant health, and the koi themselves. By nurturing this balance, you develop a greater respect for the natural world and your role in preserving it.

A Source of Pride and Inspiration

Your koi pond becomes a centerpiece of your outdoor space, a work of art that reflects your dedication and creativity. Sharing its beauty with friends and family brings a sense of pride, while the endless variety of koi colors and patterns inspires continued exploration and enjoyment.

A Lifetime of Joy

Koi keeping is not just a hobby—it's a passion that grows with you. The joy of caring for these remarkable creatures and the tranquility they bring to your life make every moment worthwhile. Whether you're a seasoned enthusiast or just starting out, the journey of koi keeping offers endless opportunities for learning, connection, and delight. Embrace the joy of koi keeping, and discover how these extraordinary fish can transform not just your pond, but your life.

40

HOW TO USE THIS GUIDE

Koi Pond Magic: Building, Stocking, and Maintaining a Healthy Koi Pond is designed to be your comprehensive companion for every step of your koi pond journey. Whether you're a beginner eager to start from scratch or an experienced enthusiast looking to refine your skills, this guide is tailored to provide clear, actionable insights. Here's how to make the most of it:

1. Start with Your Goals

Think about what you hope to achieve with your koi pond. Are you creating a tranquil backyard retreat, a showcase for prize koi, or simply exploring a new hobby? Keep your goals in mind as you navigate the guide—they'll help you focus on the most relevant sections.

2. Follow the Step-by-Step Approach

This guide is organized to take you from the basics of planning and construction to advanced koi care and pond maintenance. Each section builds on the previous one, so if you're new to koi keeping, start from the beginning to ensure you grasp the foundational knowledge.

3. Dive Into Specific Topics

For experienced koi keepers or those with specific questions, feel free to jump directly to the chapters that address your needs. Whether it's water quality management, seasonal care, or choosing koi varieties, each section is self-contained and packed with practical advice.

4. Use the Checklists and Tips

Throughout the guide, you'll find handy checklists, tips, and troubleshooting advice. These are designed to help you stay organized and avoid common pitfalls, making your koi pond journey smoother and more enjoyable.

5. Learn Through Visuals

This guide includes illustrations, diagrams, and photos to make complex concepts easy to understand. Use these visuals to clarify design ideas, equipment setup, or koi identification techniques.

6. Embrace the Seasonal Guide

Caring for koi and maintaining a healthy pond varies with the seasons. Refer to the seasonal care chapter regularly to keep your pond thriving year-round and to ensure your koi remain healthy and happy.

7. Experiment and Customize

Every koi pond is unique, reflecting its owner's vision and creativity. While this guide offers best practices, don't be afraid to adapt the advice to suit your specific environment, budget, and aesthetic preferences.

8. Use the Resources and Glossary

The appendix includes resources for sourcing koi, equipment, and plants, as well as a glossary of terms to help you navigate the world of koi keeping. Bookmark these sections for easy reference as you progress.

9. Revisit and Expand Your Knowledge

As your experience grows, revisit this guide for deeper insights or to explore advanced topics you might have skipped earlier. Koi keeping is a lifelong learning journey, and this guide is here to support you at every stage.

By following these steps, Koi Pond Magic will not only help you build and maintain a stunning koi pond but also foster a deeper connection with these remarkable fish and the serene world they inhabit. Enjoy the journey!

CHAPTER ONE

THE ART OF KOI PONDS

Koi ponds are more than just aquatic habitats; they are vibrant ecosystems and expressions of art that bring together nature, design, and tradition. In this chapter, we delve into the fascinating history of koi ponds, explore the captivating beauty and behavior of koi fish, and learn about the different koi varieties that have captured hearts worldwide.

A BRIEF HISTORY OF KOI PONDS

The origins of koi ponds can be traced back over two thousand years to China, where ornamental fish were first bred for their unique colors. This practice gained widespread popularity in Japan during the 19th century, where it evolved into the refined art of nishikigoi—the breeding of brightly colored koi. Japanese artisans meticulously cultivated koi for their vibrant patterns and symbolic significance, often incorporating them into intricately designed garden ponds. Koi ponds soon became a central feature in Japanese landscapes, representing harmony, balance, and tranquility. Over time, the appeal of koi ponds transcended cultural boundaries, becoming a global phenomenon cherished for their aesthetic beauty and calming influence. Today, they are considered both a personal retreat and a celebration of an ancient tradition.

UNDERSTANDING KOI BEAUTY, BEHAVIOR, AND SYMBOLISM

Koi fish, often referred to as "living jewels," captivate with their vivid colors, elegant movements, and endearing personalities. Beyond their aesthetic allure, koi possess fascinating behaviors and deep symbolic meaning.

• Beauty: Koi are renowned for their vibrant hues, which range from fiery reds to calming whites and shimmering metallics. Each koi's pattern is as unique as a fingerprint, making every fish a one-of-a-kind treasure.

• Behavior: Koi are intelligent and social creatures. They often recognize their caregivers and can even be trained to feed from your hand. Their gentle swimming patterns create a soothing rhythm, adding to the pond's tranquil atmosphere.

• Symbolism: In Japanese culture, koi symbolize strength, perseverance, and good fortune. The story of koi swimming upstream to become dragons reflects their association with resilience and ambition, making them a meaningful addition to any pond.

TYPES OF KOI FISH AND THEIR UNIQUE APPEAL

Koi come in a dazzling variety of colors, patterns, and scales, each with its own charm and appeal. Here are some of the most popular types:

• Kohaku: The classic koi, with striking white bodies adorned with red markings. Kohaku are prized for their simplicity and elegance.

• Showa: These koi feature a dramatic combination of black, white, and red, creating a bold and powerful visual impact.

• Sanke: Similar to Showa, Sanke koi have white bodies with red and black markings, but with no black on their heads, offering a cleaner aesthetic.

• Asagi: Known for their blue scales and red or orange bellies, Asagi koi have a serene and calming appearance.

• Ogon: Metallic koi, often in gold or platinum, that shimmer brilliantly in the water. Ogon koi symbolize wealth and prosperity.

• Butterfly Koi: Recognized for their long, flowing fins that resemble butterfly wings, adding an ethereal grace to any pond.

Each variety has its own allure, and the choice of koi allows you to personalize your pond, creating a living tapestry of color and movement. We've uncovered the rich history and timeless appeal of koi ponds, explored the beauty and symbolism of koi, and discovered the unique characteristics of various koi types. As you move forward, you'll see how these elements come together to form the foundation of your own koi pond masterpiece.

DESIGNING YOUR DREAM KOI POND

Designing a koi pond is an exciting process that allows you to blend artistry with functionality, creating a serene and visually stunning environment for both you and your koi. This chapter will guide you through the key considerations for crafting your dream koi pond, from selecting the ideal location to incorporating features like waterfalls and streams.

CHOOSING THE PERFECT LOCATION

The location of your koi pond is critical for both its aesthetic appeal and the health of your fish. Consider the following factors when selecting the perfect spot:

• Sunlight and Shade: Koi thrive in ponds with a balance of sunlight and shade. Aim for a location that receives 4-6 hours of sunlight daily. Too much sunlight can lead to overheating and algae growth, while too little may hinder plant growth and reduce koi activity.

• Visibility: Place your pond where it can be easily enjoyed from your favorite outdoor or indoor spaces. A well-placed pond becomes a natural focal point for relaxation and entertainment.

• Proximity to Utilities: Ensure the site is near an accessible water source and power supply for pumps, filters, and lighting.

• Away from Trees: Avoid placing your pond under large trees, as falling leaves can clog filters and affect water quality.

DETERMINING THE RIGHT SIZE AND DEPTH

The size and depth of your koi pond play a vital role in ensuring the health and happiness of your koi.

• Size: A larger pond provides more stable water conditions and reduces stress on your koi. For beginners, a pond of at least 1,000 gallons (approximately 10 feet long and 6 feet wide) is recommended.

• Depth: A depth of 3-4 feet is ideal. This allows koi to swim comfortably and protects them from predators and extreme temperature fluctuations. In colder climates, consider a depth of 5 feet to prevent the pond from freezing completely during winter.

POND STYLES NATURAL VS FORMAL DESIGNS

Your koi pond design sets the tone for your outdoor space and reflects your personal style. There are two primary design approaches to consider:

• Natural Designs: These ponds mimic natural landscapes, featuring irregular shapes, soft edges, and organic elements like rocks, plants, and waterfalls. Natural designs blend seamlessly with gardens and offer a tranquil, earthy feel.

• Formal Designs: Characterized by clean lines, geometric shapes, and symmetrical layouts, formal ponds exude elegance and structure. These are ideal for modern or minimalist spaces and often feature tiled or stone-lined edges.

Choose a style that complements your home's architecture and aligns with your aesthetic preferences.

Incorporating Waterfalls, Streams, and Features

Adding dynamic elements like waterfalls, streams, and decorative features enhances your pond's visual appeal and supports its ecosystem.

• Waterfalls: A cascading waterfall not only creates a stunning visual focal point but also improves aeration, keeping your water oxygen-rich and healthy for koi.

• Streams: Meandering streams add a sense of movement and natural beauty. They can also serve as an entry point for water recirculation.

• Bridges and Stones: Small bridges or stepping stones add charm and accessibility, making your pond more interactive.

• Lighting: Underwater and perimeter lighting transforms your pond into a magical nighttime feature, highlighting its beauty after sunset.

Designing your dream koi pond is about striking a balance between aesthetics, functionality, and the needs of your koi. By carefully considering location, size, style, and features, you'll create a pond that not only elevates your outdoor space but also fosters a thriving environment for your koi. In the next chapter, we'll dive into the technical aspects of pond construction and essential equipment.

CHAPTER TWO

BUILDING A KOI POND

Creating a koi pond is a rewarding project that transforms your outdoor space into a serene oasis. Whether you're taking a DIY approach or hiring professionals, this chapter provides a comprehensive guide to constructing a koi pond, including the tools, materials, and steps needed to ensure a successful build.

TOOLS AND MATERIALS NEEDED

Building a koi pond requires specific tools and materials to ensure durability, functionality, and aesthetic appeal.

Essential Tools:

• Shovels (standard and spade)

• Wheelbarrow

• Measuring tape

• Spirit level

• Utility knife

• PVC pipe cutter

• Drill and screws

Materials:

• Pond liner (EPDM or PVC)

• Underlayment for liner protection

• Pond pump and filtration system

• Skimmer and bottom drain (optional but recommended)

• Rocks, gravel, and edging materials

• UV clarifier (to reduce algae)

• Aquatic plants (for natural filtration and aesthetics)

• Water dechlorinator or pond conditioner

STEP-BY-STEP GUIDE TO POND CONSTRUCTION

Building a koi pond involves careful planning and execution. Follow these steps to bring your vision to life:

1. Plan Your Design

Sketch the desired shape and size of your pond.

Mark the pond's outline using a garden hose or spray paint.

Determine the placement of equipment like pumps and filtration systems.

2. Excavate the Pond

Dig according to your planned dimensions, ensuring varying depths for different koi activities.

Slope the edges slightly to prevent soil erosion.

Add a shelf or ledge for aquatic plants.

3. Prepare the Base

Remove sharp rocks and roots from the bottom and sides of the pond.

Lay a protective underlayment to shield the liner from punctures.

4. Install the Pond Liner

Place the liner carefully, ensuring it covers the entire pond with some overlap at the edges.

Smooth out wrinkles to prevent water flow issues.

5. Add Rocks and Edging

Arrange rocks and gravel to anchor the liner and create a natural look.

Use decorative edging materials to conceal the liner's edges.

6. Install Equipment

Position the pump, filter, and skimmer as planned.

Connect plumbing components, ensuring secure and watertight fittings.

7. Fill with Water

Gradually fill the pond with water, smoothing the liner as it settles.

Treat the water with dechlorinator or pond conditioner.

8. Test Equipment

Turn on the pump and filtration system to ensure proper functionality.

Adjust water flow and check for leaks.

Installing Liners, Pumps, and Filtration Systems

• Liners: Choose a durable, fish-safe liner like EPDM. Ensure it's large enough to cover the entire pond with extra material for securing edges.

• Pumps: Select a pump with a flow rate sufficient for your pond's size. A good rule of thumb is to circulate the entire pond volume once per hour.

• Filtration Systems: Use a combination of mechanical and biological filters to keep the water clear and healthy. Consider adding a UV clarifier for algae control.

ENSURING PROPER WATER FLOW AND CIRCULATION

Good water circulation is essential for oxygenation and waste removal.

• Position the pump to create a circular flow, directing water toward the filter and skimmer.

• Use aerators or waterfalls to boost oxygen levels.

• Avoid stagnant areas by ensuring consistent water movement throughout the pond.

TIPS FOR DIY ENTHUSIASTS VS HIRING PROFESSIONALS

For DIY Enthusiasts:

• Start with a smaller pond to gain experience.

• Watch tutorials and follow step-by-step guides like this one.

• Rent specialized equipment if needed to save costs.

For Hiring Professionals:

• Seek contractors experienced in koi pond construction.

• Discuss your vision and ensure they understand your aesthetic and functional goals.

• Hiring professionals can save time and ensure high-quality results, especially for larger or complex designs.

With careful planning and execution, building a koi pond can be a fulfilling project that enhances your outdoor space and provides a thriving home for your koi. In the next chapter, we'll explore the process of selecting and introducing koi fish to your pond, ensuring a smooth transition to their new environment.

STOCKING YOUR POND WITH KOI

Stocking your pond with koi is an exciting step that brings life and vibrancy to your carefully designed water feature. In this chapter, we'll guide you through selecting healthy koi, safely introducing them to their new home, understanding their social dynamics, and determining the right number of fish for your pond.

HOW TO SELECT HEALTHY KOI FISH

Choosing healthy koi is crucial to ensure their longevity and minimize the risk of introducing diseases into your pond.

What to Look For in Healthy Koi:

• Bright, Vibrant Colors: Healthy koi display rich and even pigmentation. Dull or faded colors may indicate poor health.

• Smooth Scales and Skin: Check for smooth, intact scales with no signs of lesions, ulcers, or parasites.

• Active Movement: Healthy koi are lively and curious, swimming confidently without lethargy or erratic behavior.

• Clear Eyes and Gills: Eyes should be clear and gills bright red, indicating good oxygenation.

• Even Body Shape: Avoid koi with noticeable deformities or asymmetry.

Where to Buy:

• Purchase from reputable koi breeders or specialized fish stores with a good track record.

• Inspect the dealer's facilities for cleanliness and the overall health of their fish stock.

• Avoid buying koi from overcrowded or poorly maintained tanks.

INTRODUCING KOI TO THEIR NEW HOME SAFELY

The transition from the dealer's tank to your pond can be stressful for koi. Follow these steps to ensure a smooth introduction:

1. Prepare the Pond:

Ensure the pond water is properly conditioned and filtered.

Test for ideal water parameters: pH (7.0–8.0), ammonia (0 ppm), nitrite (0 ppm), and nitrate (<40 ppm).

2. Acclimate the Koi:

Float the sealed transport bag in your pond for 15–30 minutes to equalize the temperature.

Gradually mix small amounts of pond water into the bag every 10 minutes to help the koi adjust to the new water chemistry.

3. Release the Koi:

Gently release the koi into the pond, avoiding sudden movements that may stress the fish.

Monitor their behavior for the first few hours to ensure they are adapting well.

UNDERSTANDING KOI SOCIAL BEHAVIOR AND HIERARCHY

Koi are social creatures with a natural inclination to form a hierarchy within their group. Understanding their behavior can help you foster a harmonious pond environment:

• Social Bonding: Koi thrive in groups and often form bonds with specific companions.

• Hierarchy: Dominance in koi ponds is typically established through mild chasing and nudging, which is normal and short-lived.

• Signs of Stress: Excessive aggression, isolation, or rapid breathing may indicate overcrowding or poor water quality.

Providing plenty of space, clean water, and hiding spots (e.g., plants or pond ornaments) can minimize conflicts and stress.

THE RIGHT NUMBER OF KOI FOR YOUR POND SIZE

Overstocking your pond can lead to poor water quality and stressed fish. Use the following guidelines to determine the appropriate number of koi for your pond:

• Standard Rule: Allow a minimum of 250 gallons of water per adult koi.

• Consider Growth: Koi can grow up to 24 inches or more, so factor in their potential size when planning.

• Filtration Capacity: Ensure your filtration system can handle the bioload of the number of koi you plan to stock.

For example:

• A 1,000-gallon pond can comfortably house 4–5 adult koi.

• A larger 3,000-gallon pond can accommodate 10–12 adult koi.

Avoid the temptation to overstock, as a smaller, well-maintained group will thrive better than an overcrowded pond.

Stocking your koi pond is a joyous occasion that marks the beginning of a vibrant, living ecosystem. By selecting healthy fish, introducing them carefully, and understanding their behavior, you'll set the foundation for a thriving pond community. In the next chapter, we'll explore how to maintain a healthy pond environment to ensure your koi continue to flourish.

CHAPTER THREE

MAINTAINING OPTIMAL WATER QUALITY

The health and well-being of your koi depend on maintaining pristine water quality in your pond. Water chemistry, oxygen levels, and proactive care are crucial for creating a stable environment. This chapter covers the fundamentals of water quality management, including understanding key water parameters, oxygenation, routine maintenance, and algae control.

Understanding Water Chemistry: pH, Nitrites, and Ammonia

Water chemistry is the cornerstone of a healthy koi pond. Familiarizing yourself with these parameters is essential:

• pH Levels:

Koi thrive in a pH range of 7.0 to 8.0.

Sudden changes in pH, known as pH swings, can stress or harm koi.

Test the pH regularly and adjust it gradually if necessary using pond-safe buffers.

• Ammonia:

Ammonia is produced by fish waste and decomposing organic matter.

Even low levels of ammonia can harm koi, causing gill damage and stress.

Ideal level: 0 ppm (parts per million). A good filtration system is key to managing ammonia.

• Nitrites and Nitrates:

Nitrites are toxic to koi, while nitrates are less harmful but can encourage algae growth if too high.

Nitrites should be at 0 ppm; nitrates should remain below 40 ppm.

Beneficial bacteria in biological filters help convert nitrites to less harmful nitrates (the nitrogen cycle).

Tip: Use a reliable water test kit to monitor these parameters weekly and after heavy rain, water changes, or adding new fish.

THE IMPORTANCE OF OXYGENATION AND AERATION

Oxygen levels play a vital role in maintaining the health of your koi and supporting beneficial bacteria in your pond's filtration system.

• Sources of Oxygen:

Waterfalls, fountains, and aerators enhance oxygen levels.

Plants contribute oxygen during the day but consume it at night, so balance is crucial.

• Signs of Low Oxygen:

Koi gasping at the surface, lethargy, and poor appetite indicate insufficient oxygen.

• Improving Oxygenation:

Install an air pump with diffusers for consistent aeration.

Increase water movement using pumps or waterfalls to boost oxygen exchange.

ROUTINE WATER CHANGES AND TESTING

Regular water changes help maintain water quality by diluting harmful compounds and replenishing essential minerals.

• Frequency and Volume:

Replace 10–20% of the pond water weekly, depending on the bioload and water quality.

Avoid large water changes, as they can disrupt the pond's balance.

• Dechlorination:

Use a pond-safe dechlorinator to neutralize chlorine and chloramines in tap water.

Test water temperature before refilling to prevent thermal shock to the koi.

• Testing Schedule:

Test water weekly for pH, ammonia, nitrites, and nitrates.

Conduct additional tests after heavy rainfall or noticeable changes in koi behavior.

ALGAE CONTROL AND PREVENTING WATER CLOUDINESS

Algae and murky water are common challenges for pond owners. While some algae are beneficial, excessive growth can affect the pond's appearance and water quality.

• Preventing Algae Overgrowth:

Limit direct sunlight by adding floating plants or shading the pond with a pergola.

Avoid overfeeding koi, as uneaten food contributes to nutrient buildup.

Use a UV clarifier to target free-floating algae that cause green water.

• Natural Algae Control:

Introduce aquatic plants like water lilies or anacharis to compete with algae for nutrients.

Encourage beneficial bacteria growth through proper filtration and aeration.

• Clearing Cloudy Water:

Address the root cause, such as poor filtration or overfeeding.

Use pond clarifiers to bind fine particles for easier removal by filters.

Maintaining optimal water quality requires consistent care, but the rewards are well worth the effort. A well-balanced pond not only supports thriving koi but also enhances the beauty of your outdoor space. In the next chapter, we'll delve into feeding your koi and understanding their dietary needs to keep them healthy and vibrant.

FEEDING YOUR KOI

Feeding your koi is not just about satisfying their hunger; it's about providing them with the right nutrients to promote growth, vitality, and long-term health. Proper nutrition is essential for koi to thrive and reach their full potential. This chapter covers the nutritional needs of koi, how to select the right food, and the best feeding practices to maintain a healthy pond ecosystem.

NUTRITIONAL REQUIREMENTS FOR HEALTHY KOI

Koi, like all living creatures, need a well-balanced diet to stay healthy. Their nutritional needs depend on their age, size, and activity level. Here's what to consider when providing the right nutrients:

• Protein:

Young koi require a higher percentage of protein (around 35–45%) for growth.

Adult koi need a more moderate protein intake (around 30–35%) to maintain a healthy body condition.

Protein helps with tissue repair, growth, and immune function.

• Fats:

Fats are an important source of energy and help with the absorption of fat-soluble vitamins.

Choose foods with healthy fats like omega-3 and omega-6 fatty acids, which promote vibrant colors and immune health.

• Carbohydrates:

Koi need carbohydrates for energy, but they should not make up the majority of their diet. Excess carbs can lead to obesity and water quality issues due to uneaten food.

• Vitamins and Minerals:

A well-balanced koi diet should include essential vitamins (like A, D, E, and C) and minerals (like calcium and magnesium) to support immune health, color, and bone structure.

Ensure your koi food contains trace minerals to boost overall vitality.

• Fiber:

Fiber helps with digestion and prevents constipation. Koi benefit from foods that contain plant matter or natural fiber sources.

CHOOSING THE RIGHT FOOD PELLETS, TREATS, AND SEASONAL DIETS

Selecting the right food for your koi is essential for their overall health. Here's a breakdown of common koi food types and how to choose the best option:

• Pellets:

Pellets are the most common and convenient form of koi food. Choose sinking pellets for younger koi or floating pellets for adults.

Look for pellets with high-quality ingredients such as fish meal, krill, or algae. Avoid foods with excessive fillers like corn or wheat.

Opt for floating pellets if you want to monitor how much your koi are eating, as they are easier to spot and remove if uneaten.

• Treats:

Occasional treats like worms, shrimp, or fruits (such as watermelon and strawberries) can add variety to your koi's diet and encourage interaction with you.

Treats should be given sparingly to avoid overfeeding, which can lead to water quality issues.

• Seasonal Diets:

In the warmer months, koi have higher metabolic rates and require more protein to support their growth and energy.

In colder months (below 50°F or 10°C), koi enter a state of reduced activity, so their metabolism slows down. At this time, they require a lower-protein diet, typically in the form of wheat germ food that is easy to digest.

As the weather warms, gradually switch back to higher-protein foods.

FEEDING SCHEDULES AND QUANTITY RECOMMENDATIONS

Feeding your koi correctly is as important as choosing the right food. Here's a guide to ensure your koi are properly nourished without overfeeding:

• Feeding Frequency:

During the warmer months, feed koi 2–3 times a day, depending on their size and activity level.

In winter or during colder months, reduce feeding frequency to once or twice a week, or stop feeding entirely if the water temperature drops below 50°F (10°C).

• Quantity Recommendations:

A general rule of thumb is to feed your koi as much as they can eat in 5–10 minutes.

Use the "two-minute rule": feed your koi and watch them for two minutes. If there's still food floating after that time, remove the excess.

Avoid overfeeding, as uneaten food can decay, leading to poor water quality.

• Adjusting for Growth:

As koi grow, their feeding needs increase. Monitor their weight and adjust their food portions accordingly.

COMMON FEEDING MISTAKES TO AVOID

While feeding koi is straightforward, there are a few common mistakes to avoid:

1. Overfeeding:

Overfeeding can lead to poor water quality, increased algae growth, and obesity in koi. Stick to the "5-minute rule" and remove excess food if necessary.

2. Feeding the Wrong Foods:

Avoid feeding koi low-quality food or items that are not nutritionally balanced. Koi require food that is specifically formulated for their needs.

3. Feeding Too Often in Cold Weather:

Do not feed koi during the winter months when water temperatures are low. Feeding in cold water can lead to digestive problems since koi's metabolic rate is much slower in cooler temperatures.

4. Not Adjusting Diet for Growth:

As koi mature, their nutritional needs change. Make sure to adjust their food to support their size and developmental stage.

5. Feeding in Dirty Water:

Never feed koi if the water quality is poor. Uneaten food can exacerbate water quality problems. Always check water parameters before feeding.

By understanding your koi's dietary needs and implementing a thoughtful feeding routine, you'll ensure that your fish stay healthy, vibrant, and active. Proper nutrition also plays a key role in the koi's immune system, which is critical for preventing disease. In the next chapter, we'll discuss common health issues in koi and how to keep them in top condition throughout the year.

LANDSCAPING AROUND YOUR POND

Landscaping around your koi pond is an essential step in creating an inviting, harmonious space while also contributing to the overall health of the pond ecosystem. Thoughtfully chosen plants, as well as protective measures, not only enhance the beauty of your pond but also support water quality and koi health. This chapter explores how to integrate landscaping features like plants, native flora, and predator prevention to achieve a balanced and thriving pond environment.

ADDING PLANTS FOR SHADE AND BEAUTY

Plants are essential for both the aesthetic appeal and the health of your koi pond. By strategically placing plants around and in the pond, you can create a stunning visual effect while offering shade for your koi and reducing the risk of algae growth. Here's how to use plants effectively:

• Shading Your Pond:

Shade helps cool the water, reduce algae growth, and provide a natural retreat for koi, especially during the hottest months.

Floating plants like water lilies and lotus are perfect for shading large areas of the pond's surface. Their leaves provide shelter for koi and help keep the water cooler.

You can also plant marginal plants around the edges of your pond, such as water iris or papyrus, which can partially shade the water without overcrowding the pond.

• Aesthetic Appeal:

Consider a variety of plants that bloom in different seasons to maintain color and interest throughout the year.

Water lilies provide large, beautiful flowers, while lotus add an elegant touch to deeper areas of the pond. Marginal plants like water mint or pickerel rush can create a natural, wild look around the edges.

For visual interest, use aquatic grasses like rushes and sedges that add texture and movement to the pond.

AQUATIC PLANTS FOR NATURAL FILTRATION

Aquatic plants play a critical role in maintaining the health of your koi pond by acting as natural filters. They help remove excess nutrients from the water, absorb harmful substances, and prevent algae overgrowth. Here's how to select and incorporate aquatic plants into your pond for filtration purposes:

• Floating Plants:

Water lettuce, duckweed, and water hyacinth are excellent at absorbing excess nutrients and shading the water surface.

These plants float on the surface, blocking sunlight from reaching algae and absorbing nitrates and phosphates from the water.

• Submerged Plants:

Plants like anacharis or hornwort grow beneath the surface and help oxygenate the water while also absorbing nutrients that algae might otherwise use.

Submerged plants are particularly effective at preventing algae blooms by reducing nutrient levels in the pond.

• Marginal Plants:

Plants like water lilies and cattails grow at the edges and can be placed in shallow water. Their roots help filter the water by absorbing excess nutrients, and their large leaves provide shade for the koi.

• Benefits of Plant Filtration:

By using aquatic plants for filtration, you reduce your reliance on mechanical filtration systems and create a more natural, balanced pond ecosystem.

Plants provide natural oxygenation, reduce chemical imbalances, and improve water clarity, making them an essential part of pond maintenance.

CREATING A HARMONIOUS ECOSYSTEM WITH NATIVE FLORA

Incorporating native plants into your pond's landscaping helps maintain a balanced ecosystem and supports local wildlife. Native flora thrives in the natural climate and contributes to the pond's overall health by supporting local species and providing natural food sources. Here's how to integrate native plants effectively:

• Why Choose Native Plants?

Native plants are well-suited to your region's climate and water conditions, meaning they require less maintenance and are more resistant to pests and diseases.

They also provide important habitats for local wildlife, such as birds, insects, and amphibians, while helping maintain the natural biodiversity of the area.

• Popular Native Aquatic Plants:

Water lilies and lotus are often native to many regions and add both beauty and function to the pond.

Bulrushes and cattails are native marginals that help absorb nutrients and filter water.

Pickerel rush and Arrowhead can be planted along the edges of your pond to create a natural and cohesive look while helping with water filtration.

• Creating a Balanced Ecosystem:

Incorporating a variety of native plants helps ensure your pond remains balanced and resilient. A mix of floating, submerged, and marginal plants will create a well-rounded system where plants naturally support each other.

Native plants also contribute to stabilizing pond banks and improving water clarity by reducing erosion.

PROTECTING YOUR POND FROM PREDATORS

While koi ponds are beautiful and serene, they can also attract predators, such as birds, raccoons, and even stray animals looking for an easy meal. Implementing protective measures will ensure your koi remain safe from harm. Here are ways to safeguard your pond and koi from potential threats:

• Bird Predators:

Herons, egrets, and other large birds can be major threats to koi. Installing a netting system over your pond or using a predator-proof cover can help keep birds at bay.

Decoys, such as plastic herons or reflective objects (e.g., shiny tape), can also deter predatory birds.

Another effective method is placing tall plants and rocks around the pond to provide hiding spots for koi.

• Raccoon and Animal Deterrents:

Raccoons and other nocturnal predators can be a problem, especially at night. Fencing around the pond with a high barrier (3–4 feet) can prevent them from accessing the water.

Motion-sensor lights and sprinklers can help deter raccoons and other animals that might be attracted to the pond.

Install pond alarms or use motion detectors to alert you when an animal is near the pond.

• Protective Fencing:

Surrounding your pond with a low fence can keep out large animals while allowing easy access for you and your koi. A decently sized ledge or bordering plants can also act as a barrier without obstructing the pond's beauty.

By landscaping with both beauty and functionality in mind, you can enhance the aesthetic appeal of your pond while creating a more balanced and self-sustaining environment for your koi. Thoughtfully placed plants, native flora, and protective measures all contribute to the well-being of your pond, its inhabitants, and the surrounding ecosystem. In the next chapter, we'll discuss seasonal pond care and how to adjust your pond management practices throughout the year.

CHAPTER FOUR

SEASONAL CARE FOR YOUR KOI POND

Maintaining your koi pond throughout the seasons requires attention to changing weather conditions and the needs of both your pond and its inhabitants. Each season brings unique challenges and opportunities for enhancing the pond's health and appearance. This chapter will guide you through the essential steps to take for winter, spring, summer, and fall to ensure your koi thrive year-round.

PREPARING YOUR POND FOR WINTER

As winter approaches, koi and other pond life need special care to ensure they remain healthy and comfortable through colder months. Freezing temperatures can pose risks to the pond's ecosystem, so proper preparation is key.

• Stop Feeding Koi:

As water temperatures fall below 50°F (10°C), koi enter a state of dormancy and stop eating. Any food offered at this time can decompose in the water, leading to harmful chemical imbalances.

Gradually reduce feeding as the water temperature decreases, and stop feeding completely when the temperature hits 50°F.

• Check Pond Equipment:

Turn off pumps and filters when the water temperature drops below 50°F to prevent them from freezing or breaking.

Remove debris from the pond, such as leaves and plant material, as decomposing organic matter can cause water quality issues during winter.

Consider installing a de-icer to prevent the water from freezing completely. This will create a hole in the ice, allowing gases to escape and preventing suffocation of the koi.

• Cover the Pond:

Use a pond cover or netting to protect the water from falling debris like leaves and twigs, which can disrupt the pond's balance.

Keep the cover loose to allow air circulation and prevent overheating from trapped sunlight.

SPRING CLEANING AND RESTARTING THE POND SYSTEM

Spring is the time for renewal and fresh growth, both for your koi pond and the pond's ecosystem. Cleaning and restarting your system properly will ensure a smooth transition from the cold months and set the stage for a healthy pond season ahead.

• Clean the Pond:

Remove winter debris that may have accumulated, such as fallen leaves, dead plant matter, or leftover food remnants.

Use a pond vacuum or net to clean the bottom of the pond, removing muck and sludge that could affect water quality.

Trim back plants that may have died off over winter or that have overgrown, ensuring new growth can thrive.

• Restart the Filtration System:

Before restarting your pump and filtration system, check that all components are in good working order. Clean or replace any filter media that may have accumulated with dirt or debris.

Turn on the pump and allow water to circulate through the system before reintroducing koi to ensure proper filtration and water flow.

• Check Water Chemistry:

Test the water for ammonia, nitrites, nitrates, and pH levels. Winter months can lead to imbalances, so this is an ideal time to make necessary adjustments.

Add beneficial bacteria to kickstart the filtration system, which helps break down organic waste and improves water quality.

• Reintroduce Koi:

After the water temperature stabilizes and is consistently above 50°F, you can safely reintroduce koi to the pond.

Ensure the water temperature is similar to that of the container you've kept the koi in, to avoid shocking them.

MANAGING HEAT AND EVAPORATION IN SUMMER

The summer months bring warmth and sunshine, but extreme heat can also lead to challenges for your koi and the pond system. Proper care and management during the summer will help maintain optimal conditions for your koi.

• Ensure Adequate Oxygenation:

During hot weather, oxygen levels in the water can drop, especially if the pond surface is covered with algae or organic debris. Ensure that your pump and filtration system are running effectively to provide adequate oxygenation.

Consider adding air stones or a pond aerator to enhance oxygen levels and keep the water circulating.

• Manage Water Temperature:

Ideally, koi thrive in water temperatures between 65°F and 75°F (18°C to 24°C). If the temperature rises above 80°F (27°C), consider using a shade structure like floating plants, a pond canopy, or even a shade sail to provide relief from the sun.

You can also adjust the placement of large rocks or other features to create shaded areas in the pond.

• Prevent Overheating:

In addition to shading, you can also reduce feeding in summer. Koi have slower digestion in warm water, so overfeeding can cause uneaten food to deteriorate and degrade water quality.

Use a water chiller if you live in an area with extreme summer temperatures. This can regulate the water temperature and ensure your koi stay comfortable.

• Control Evaporation:

Evaporation can be a concern in hot weather, particularly if your pond is shallow or has a large surface area. Adding dechlorinated water to top off the pond may be necessary.

Use pond covers to reduce evaporation, especially during heatwaves. However, ensure that the cover does not block airflow, as this could reduce oxygen levels.

FALL MAINTENANCE REMOVING LEAVES AND DEBRIS

As the weather cools down in fall, it's crucial to prepare your pond for the upcoming winter. The fall season brings falling leaves and debris that can quickly accumulate in your pond. Here are key maintenance steps to take in the fall:

• Remove Fallen Leaves:

Fallen leaves can decompose in the pond, leading to increased organic matter that can affect water quality and oxygen levels. Use a pond net or skimmer to regularly remove leaves before they sink and decompose.

Trimming back any overgrown plants and removing dead plant matter can also help prevent debris from cluttering the pond.

• Check Water Levels:

Fall winds can cause evaporation, so check water levels regularly. Keep your pond topped up with dechlorinated water to ensure your filtration system remains effective.

• Prepare for Winter:

Before the first frost, ensure that all pond equipment is in working order for the upcoming cold months. Clean and store any equipment that will not be in use over the winter.

Install or check your de-icer and consider using pond netting to protect against fallen leaves.

By managing seasonal changes with proper pond care, you will ensure a thriving, healthy environment for your koi year-round. Regular maintenance, along with a proactive approach to water quality and temperature control, will help you overcome seasonal challenges and keep your pond flourishing through every weather shift.

KOI HEALTH AND DISEASE PREVENTION

Maintaining the health of your koi is essential for a thriving pond ecosystem. Koi are generally resilient, but they are still susceptible to illness, stress, and disease if proper care is not given. This chapter will help you recognize early signs of distress, identify common koi diseases, and provide steps to ensure your fish stay healthy, happy, and stress-free.

RECOGNIZING SIGNS OF ILLNESS OR STRESS

Koi are naturally good at hiding illness, so early detection is crucial for effective treatment. Stress and illness can lead to weakened immune systems, making koi more susceptible to infections and diseases. Understanding how to spot signs of distress will help you address problems before they escalate.

• Changes in Behavior:

Lethargy or lack of movement can indicate illness or stress. Healthy koi are usually active, swimming around their pond.

Erratic swimming behavior, such as swimming in circles, near the surface, or rubbing against objects in the pond, is often a sign of discomfort or irritation.

Excessive surface breathing can signal oxygen depletion, poor water quality, or respiratory issues.

• Physical Symptoms:

Abnormal coloring (such as fading or darkening) may indicate health problems like infections or environmental stress.

Skin lesions, ulcers, or unusual growths can be signs of bacterial infections or parasites.

Fins held tightly against the body could indicate a parasite infestation or stress.

Clamped gills or difficulty breathing is another warning sign of poor water quality or respiratory distress.

• Feeding Issues:

Loss of appetite or refusal to eat is often a first indicator of stress or illness, especially if it persists over several days.

COMMON KOI DISEASES AND TREATMENTS

Koi are susceptible to various diseases, ranging from parasitic infections to bacterial problems. Understanding these common diseases and knowing how to treat them can help you protect your koi from harm.

• Ich (Ichthyophthirius Multifiliis):

Symptoms: White spots on the skin, fins, and gills.

Treatment: Use a medicated bath or add a formalin or salt treatment to the pond. Increasing water temperature slightly can also speed up the parasite's life cycle and help eradicate it faster.

• Koi Herpesvirus (KHV):

Symptoms: Lethargy, ulcers, lesions, and sudden death.

Treatment: KHV has no cure, and affected fish must be isolated immediately to prevent the spread. It is crucial to quarantine any new koi before introducing them to the pond.

• Fin Rot:

Symptoms: Fraying or blackened fins, often caused by poor water quality or injury.

Treatment: Improve water conditions, remove affected fish, and use a broad-spectrum antibiotic or topical treatments.

• Dropsy:

Symptoms: Swelling of the abdomen, raised scales, and lethargy.

Treatment: Dropsy is often a symptom of internal infections. Isolate the fish and use antibiotics or salt baths for treatment.

• External Parasites (e.g., Costia, Trichodina, and Chilodonella):

Symptoms: Excessive rubbing, rapid gill movement, and mucous coating.

Treatment: Use parasite-specific treatments, such as formalin or copper sulfate, and consider using a UV clarifier to help reduce parasite load in the pond.

• Columnaris:

Symptoms: Lesions around the mouth or fins that appear cottony.

Treatment: Use antibiotics such as oxytetracycline or salt baths to treat the infection.

QUARANTINE PROCEDURES FOR NEW FISH

Introducing new koi into your pond is an exciting process, but it also brings the risk of introducing disease or parasites. Quarantining new koi is a crucial step in preventing the spread of illnesses to your existing fish.

• Set Up a Quarantine Tank:

Use a separate tank or pond that is well-aerated, has a filtration system, and is equipped with appropriate water temperature and pH.

Ensure that the quarantine tank is spacious enough for the koi to swim comfortably for a period of at least 2-4 weeks.

• Monitor and Inspect:

During quarantine, carefully monitor the fish for any signs of illness or stress. Look for unusual behavior, skin lesions, or changes in eating habits.

Perform regular water tests to ensure that the quarantine tank remains stable, as poor water quality can stress the fish and lead to illness.

• Treat Preventively:

Even if the new koi appear healthy, consider treating them with a mild antibacterial or antiparasitic medication to prevent hidden infections from spreading.

Avoid mixing quarantine water with your main pond water to prevent contamination.

• Avoid Overcrowding:

Quarantining multiple new koi in the same tank can stress the fish, making them more susceptible to illness. It's best to quarantine koi in small groups or individually.

TIPS FOR KEEPING KOI STRESS-FREE AND HEALTHY

Stress is a major contributing factor to illness in koi, and maintaining a calm, healthy environment is essential for their well-being. By addressing the underlying causes of stress and creating a stable, safe environment, you can reduce the chances of disease outbreaks.

• Maintain Consistent Water Quality:

Stress often occurs due to fluctuating water conditions. Make sure to regularly test and adjust water parameters, such as pH, ammonia, nitrites, and nitrates, to maintain balance.

Proper filtration and aeration are key to keeping the water oxygenated and clear.

• Avoid Overcrowding:

Too many koi in a small pond can lead to stress, competition for food, and poor water quality.

Follow guidelines for the appropriate number of koi based on pond size and allow enough space for each fish to thrive.

• Minimize Handling:

Koi can become stressed by frequent handling, which can also introduce contaminants into the pond. Avoid unnecessary netting or contact with the fish unless it's necessary for health checks or treatments.

• Provide Hiding Spots:

Koi are social but also need a place to hide and rest. Provide rock formations, floating plants, or pond caves where koi can retreat and feel safe from predators or disturbances.

• Regular Monitoring:

Keep an eye on your koi's behavior and appearance daily. Early detection of stress or illness is crucial to preventing serious health issues.

By following these practices for health management, you can prevent diseases and ensure that your koi remain vibrant and beautiful for many years. Regular attention to water quality, quarantine procedures, and minimizing stress will go a long way in protecting the health of your koi and keeping your pond ecosystem in harmony.

CHAPTER FIVE

ENHANCING YOUR KOI POND EXPERIENCE

Creating a koi pond is not just about maintaining a healthy aquatic environment for your fish; it's also about crafting an immersive space that enhances your enjoyment of the pond. By adding thoughtful features, you can transform your koi pond into a tranquil retreat, an eye-catching garden centerpiece, or even a gathering spot for friends and family. This chapter explores how to elevate your koi pond experience with lighting, landscaping, feeding stations, and more.

ADDING LIGHTING FOR EVENING AMBIANCE

One of the most magical ways to enhance your koi pond is by incorporating lighting. Lighting can create a serene atmosphere during the evening, allowing you to enjoy your pond long after the sun sets. It can also highlight the natural beauty of your koi and the surrounding landscape.

• Underwater Lighting:

Use submersible LED lights to illuminate the pond from within. These lights can create a beautiful glow, highlighting the movements of your koi and the natural features of your pond.

Ensure that the lights are waterproof and designed for underwater use to prevent electrical hazards.

A soft, warm light often works best for creating a calming, ambient atmosphere, while brighter lights can draw attention to specific features or fish.

• Accent Lighting Around the Pond:

Placing spotlights or floodlights around the perimeter of your pond can help create dramatic effects, casting light on plants, rocks, or waterfalls.

Low-voltage garden lights or solar-powered lamps are an energy-efficient way to light pathways and surrounding plants, giving your pond area a subtle, elegant glow.

• Floating Lights:

Floating lanterns or small LED floats placed on the surface of the pond can add a whimsical touch and complement the natural movement of the water.

• Timing:

Install a timer for your lighting system to automatically turn on at dusk and off at dawn, saving energy and ensuring that the lighting enhances the natural rhythms of the day and night.

BUILDING BRIDGES, SEATING, AND PATHWAYS

Enhancing your koi pond experience goes beyond the water and fish; it's about creating an inviting space around the pond that allows you to enjoy the view and connect with nature. Thoughtfully designed bridges, seating areas, and pathways not only improve the aesthetic appeal of the pond but also provide a functional way to enjoy your space.

• Bridges:

A wooden or stone bridge can add a rustic, charming element to your pond and provide a great vantage point to observe your koi from above. Bridges also create a sense of movement within the landscape, drawing visitors' eyes across the water.

When selecting materials, consider the durability and natural look of the materials in your pond's design. Opt for weather-resistant wood or stone that blends in with the natural surroundings.

• Seating Areas:

Add comfortable seating like benches, chairs, or lounge areas near the pond to create a relaxing spot where you can watch your koi and enjoy the tranquility of the pond. Consider using materials like teak, which is both weather-resistant and elegant.

Position the seating where you can see the koi clearly but are not directly in their path, allowing you to enjoy the view without disturbing the fish.

• Pathways:

Build stone or gravel pathways around your pond to make it easy to move around the area. These pathways can connect the pond to other areas of your garden, inviting guests to stroll and enjoy the scenery.

Choose materials that blend with your pond's design, such as natural stone, cobblestone, or flagstone. Adding lighting along the path can create a beautiful effect, guiding the way as the evening falls.

INCORPORATING FISH FEEDING STATIONS

Feeding koi is one of the most enjoyable parts of koi keeping, and creating a dedicated feeding station can make this experience even more special. A feeding station is not only practical but can also become a focal point in your pond.

• Automatic Feeders:

If you're looking for convenience, consider installing an automatic fish feeder that dispenses food at regular intervals. These can be programmed to feed your koi several times a day, ensuring that they receive the right amount of food even when you're not around.

Automatic feeders also help reduce overfeeding and maintain water quality by controlling the amount of food dispensed.

• Hand-Feeding Stations:

Set up a dedicated area by placing rocks or stepping stones in a specific part of your pond to encourage koi to gather in one location for feeding.

You can also build a small platform or floating dock where you can sit and hand-feed your koi. Not only is this enjoyable for you, but it can help form a bond with your koi over time.

• Feeding Stations for Observation:

A well-placed feeding station can provide an excellent spot for observing your koi. Watch as they eagerly gather around for food, displaying their natural behavior and feeding habits. Adding a small floating platform or feeding tray will keep food in a specific area, making it easier to see your koi in action.

HOSTING KOI POND TOURS OR COMPETITIONS

For koi enthusiasts, sharing your pond with others can be an exciting and rewarding experience. Hosting koi pond tours or even competitions can be a great way to engage with the community and show off your hard work.

• Koi Pond Tours:

Invite local garden clubs, koi enthusiasts, or friends to visit your pond during a tour. Organize your pond and surrounding garden for easy viewing and provide information on your koi, their care, and the design of the pond.

Use informational signs or brochures to educate visitors about koi care and the specifics of maintaining a healthy pond. This is a great opportunity to share your knowledge and passion with others.

• Koi Competitions:

Participate in or host a koi competition where you can showcase the beauty and health of your koi. These events often include judging criteria such as size, color, body shape, and fin quality.

Not only do competitions provide recognition for your koi-keeping efforts, but they also connect you with other passionate koi enthusiasts.

Enhancing your koi pond experience is about creating a space where you can enjoy both the aesthetic beauty of your pond and the therapeutic qualities it brings. By adding thoughtful features such as lighting, seating, feeding stations, and sharing your passion with others through tours or competitions, you can elevate the enjoyment of your koi pond for years to come.

TROUBLESHOOTING AND FAQS

Even with the best care, koi ponds can sometimes present challenges. Whether it's water quality issues, behavioral concerns with your koi, or structural problems, being prepared with knowledge can help you resolve these issues quickly and effectively. In this chapter, we'll address some of the most common pond-related problems and provide practical solutions to keep your pond and koi healthy.

Why Is My Pond Water Green or Cloudy?

One of the most common complaints koi pond owners face is green or cloudy water. This problem can be caused by several factors, and understanding the root cause is essential for fixing it.

• Algae Growth:

Green water is often caused by a bloom of suspended algae. This algae thrives when there is an excess of nutrients, typically from uneaten food, fish waste, or decaying organic matter.

Solution:

Reduce nutrient levels: Regular cleaning of the pond and removing debris from the bottom can help. Ensure you're not overfeeding your koi.

Increase filtration: Make sure your pond's filtration system is strong enough for the pond's size. A UV sterilizer can also help by killing algae in the water.

Add more plants: Aquatic plants can naturally absorb excess nutrients, which will help reduce algae growth.

Partial water changes: Regularly replacing 10-15% of the water each week can help maintain clearer water.

• Cloudy Water from Suspended Particles:

Cloudiness can also be caused by fine debris or organic matter suspended in the water, often due to improper filtration or too much organic material.

Solution:

Improve filtration: Ensure your filtration system is working properly and is adequate for your pond size. You may need to upgrade or add additional filtration if your pond is heavily stocked.

Check water chemistry: Imbalances in pH or ammonia levels can exacerbate cloudiness, so test your water regularly and adjust as needed.

HOW TO FIX A LEAKING POND

A leaking pond can be frustrating, but the good news is that most leaks are fixable with the right approach. Leaks typically occur in the pond liner or at the joints where different materials meet. Here's how to address the issue:

• Step 1: Identify the Leak

The first step is to find the source of the leak. If you suspect a liner leak, inspect the pond carefully for any visible holes or tears. You can also perform a bucket test: fill the pond to a certain level, mark it with a water line, and monitor the level over time. If the water level drops noticeably, there's a leak.

Check around the edges of the pond and any areas where pipes or hoses enter the pond, as these are common points of failure.

• Step 2: Repair the Leak

For Liner Leaks:

If the leak is in a rubber liner, patch it with a pond liner repair kit, which can be found at most garden stores. Clean the area around the tear thoroughly, apply the patch, and press it down firmly. Allow the patch to cure for 24 hours before refilling the pond.

For Rigid Liners: A flexible pond sealant or epoxy resin can be used to seal cracks or holes. Be sure to follow the manufacturer's instructions carefully for the best results.

For Pipe Leaks:

If the leak is in a pipe or hose, tighten the fittings, or replace any damaged sections. You can also use waterproof tape or a pipe sealant to temporarily fix minor leaks. If the pipe is cracked, it may need to be replaced.

• Step 3: Monitor the Repair

After you've made the repairs, monitor the water level over the next few days. If the leak persists, recheck the area and apply additional sealant if necessary.

WHAT TO DO IF KOI ARE JUMPING OR HIDING

Koi are naturally curious and peaceful fish, but if they're suddenly exhibiting strange behaviors like jumping out of the water or hiding, it may indicate an underlying problem. Understanding the potential causes and knowing how to respond is key to ensuring their health and safety.

• Jumping:

Cause 1 - Poor Water Quality:

If the water quality is poor, with high levels of ammonia, nitrites, or low oxygen, koi may jump as a way to escape the discomfort.

Solution: Test the water regularly and ensure that the filtration system is running efficiently. Consider adding an air pump or increasing oxygenation if needed.

Cause 2 - Overcrowding or Stress:

If the pond is overcrowded or if there's insufficient space, koi may become stressed and jump to escape.

Solution: Check your pond's stocking density. Overcrowding can lead to health problems and stress for your koi, so ensure that your pond is appropriately sized for the number of fish.

• Hiding:

Cause 1 - Illness or Injury:

If a koi is hiding, it may be feeling unwell or injured. Koi tend to isolate themselves when they are not feeling their best.

Solution: Check for signs of illness such as lesions, discoloration, or abnormal swimming patterns. If you notice any, quarantine the affected fish and seek treatment.

Cause 2 - Environmental Changes:

Koi may also hide if there's a significant environmental change, such as sudden temperature shifts or loud noises.

Solution: Make sure the water temperature remains stable and try to minimize disruptions around the pond.

ANSWERS TO COMMON BEGINNER QUESTIONS

• How often should I feed my koi?

During warmer months, feed your koi 2-3 times a day, offering only what they can eat in 5 minutes. In colder months, when koi's metabolism slows, reduce feeding frequency. Always monitor the water quality to avoid overfeeding.

• How do I know if my koi are happy?

Healthy koi exhibit bright colors, active swimming, and good appetite. They should swim freely and engage with their environment. Watch for signs of stress, such as lethargy, erratic swimming, or refusal to eat.

• Why are my koi not eating?

There are several possible reasons, including water quality issues, temperature changes, or stress. Make sure the water parameters are optimal and ensure the pond is free of pollutants. If the temperature is too cold, koi's appetite may decrease naturally.

• What's the best way to clean the pond?

Regular maintenance is key. Remove debris from the pond surface, clean the filter regularly, and perform partial water changes every 2-4 weeks. In spring, consider doing a deeper cleaning to remove accumulated organic matter from the bottom of the pond. By understanding the common issues koi pond owners face and knowing how to address them, you can ensure that your koi remain healthy and your pond stays beautiful for years to come. Troubleshooting and resolving issues early on will allow you to enjoy your koi pond experience without the stress of avoidable problems.

CELEBRATING YOUR KOI POND SUCCESS

Building and maintaining a koi pond is not just a hobby—it's a journey of creativity, patience, and dedication. As you've learned throughout this guide, the process of designing, building, stocking, and caring for your koi pond involves numerous steps, each contributing to the creation of a serene aquatic paradise. From choosing the right location and constructing the perfect pond, to stocking it with vibrant koi and ensuring the health of both your fish and your water, every decision you make helps bring your vision to life.

Now, as you stand back and admire the beauty of your koi swimming gracefully through clear waters, it's time to reflect on the success you've achieved. Your koi pond is a testament to your hard work and commitment to creating a space that nurtures not only your koi but also your own well-being. Whether it's the peacefulness you feel while watching your koi glide through the water or the joy of seeing your fish thrive, the reward is well worth the effort.

THE TRANQUILITY AND FULFILLMENT OF KOI KEEPING

Koi keeping offers more than just the satisfaction of having a beautiful pond; it brings a profound sense of tranquility and fulfillment. The gentle movement of koi and the soothing sounds of flowing water can provide a peaceful retreat from the demands of daily life. Many koi keepers describe the experience as meditative—a way to reconnect with nature and escape the stresses of the world.

The daily tasks of maintaining water quality, feeding your koi, and observing their behavior create a routine that fosters mindfulness. The bond you develop with your koi, watching them grow, change, and thrive in their environment, can be incredibly rewarding. There's also something deeply fulfilling about seeing your koi pond evolve into a flourishing ecosystem, complete with plants, wildlife, and a variety of aquatic life. For many koi enthusiasts, the hobby becomes a lifelong pursuit, one that brings constant learning and growth. As you continue to care for your pond and its inhabitants, you'll discover new ways to improve and enjoy your pond, whether through adding new features, experimenting with different koi varieties, or perfecting your pond maintenance techniques.

INSPIRING STORIES FROM THE KOI COMMUNITY

Koi keeping has a way of bringing together people from all walks of life, creating a tight-knit community of passionate individuals. Across the globe, koi enthusiasts share their experiences, exchange knowledge, and inspire each other to improve their ponds and koi care practices. Many koi keepers start as beginners, eager to create their own beautiful ponds, but over time, they become experts in the field, sharing their journey with others. One inspiring story comes from a koi keeper in Japan who, after years of careful breeding and pond management, succeeded in raising a koi fish that won multiple international awards. This koi, once a small, unassuming fish, became a symbol of dedication and passion—an achievement not just for the individual keeper, but for the entire koi community. Similarly, many koi keepers have overcome challenges such as poor water quality, fish diseases, or predators. These stories remind us that koi keeping is a journey of persistence and resilience. Through trial and error, and with a deep commitment to the health and happiness of their fish, many enthusiasts find themselves rewarded with a thriving pond and a stronger connection to nature. Sharing these stories not only motivates other koi keepers but also helps spread the knowledge and wisdom accumulated over years of experience. Whether through local koi clubs, online forums, or social media, the koi community is full of individuals eager to offer advice, share their experiences, and inspire others to take the leap into the world of koi keeping.

As you celebrate the success of your koi pond, remember that the rewards are not just in the aesthetic beauty of your pond, but in the serenity, fulfillment, and sense of community that comes with being a koi keeper. Your pond is a living testament to your care, effort, and passion, and with each passing year, it will continue to evolve, just like you. Here's to many more years of joyful koi keeping and the endless tranquility your pond provides.